The Book of James: Sermons and Renderings

Rev. Dana Vaughn

Parson's Porch Books

www.parsonsporchbooks.com

The Book of James: Sermons and Renderings

ISBN: Softcover 978-1-949888-67-6

Copyright © 2019 by Dana Vaughn

All rights reserved. No part of this book may be reproduced or transmitted in any form or by any means, electronic or mechanical, including photocopying, recording, or by any information storage and retrieval system, without permission in writing from the publisher.

The Book of James:
Sermons and Renderings

Table of Contents

Being Doers, Not Merely Hearers 7
   James 1:17-27 7
No Partiality 20
   James 2:1-10; 14-18
The Power of Words 35
   James 3:1-12
Submit Yourselves 50
   James 3:13-4:3;7-8a
Pray Y'all 63
   James 5:3-20

Being Doers, Not Merely Hearers
James 1:17-27

As we begin with this first chapter of James, we are starting a 5 week-long series on the book of James.

So, for the next several weeks we will be diving a little bit deeper into this book. Taking a closer look at who James was, what James had to say, and how that relates to our present everyday lives.

As we begin our series, we began by hearing the second half of chapter 1, in the book of James.

In the second half of chapter 1, James goes into much detail about how we are **to be doers of God's word, not just merely listeners, and not just merely hearers** of God's word and Christ's teachings. That is to say that, as Christians, as disciples of Christ, we are not to let the teachings of Christ or God's word fall on deaf ears.

We are encouraged to embody Christ's teachings. We are encouraged to go out into the world and witness to others. We are encouraged to go out and minister to those who need it the most. Or to quote the words of James, we are told to go out into the world and "care for the widows and the orphans."

Let us not interpret the words of James too narrowly when he says, widows and orphans.

Let us not limit those terms to a very specific group of individuals. For it may mean and include, your father or mother, your husband or wife. It may mean and include your grandmother or grandfather, or your best friend who is suffering. Those terms refer to anyone who is alone, oppressed, or in need of your care and compassion.

The point that James was trying to make was that we are to be out there caring for others and out there doing, rather than sitting at home talking about doing.

Many Christians find the book of James off-putting for this reason. They find it off-putting because the entire book is a call to action. Many people find it challenging because it presents 60 obligations, or 60 admonishments in only a short 108 verses.

Within those 108 verses, throughout the entire book of James, James focuses on the truths of Jesus' words that were delivered on the Sermon on the Mount. James pulls from those teachings and motivates us, and calls us to act upon what Jesus was teaching when He delivered the Sermon on the Mount.

Throughout the book of James, he contends that faith produces authentic deeds. In other words, if those who call themselves God's people truly belong to Him, then their lives will produce deeds of fruit. They will produce actions.

In this book, James rails against the hypocritical believers who say one thing but then go and do another. He is speaking to those who say they are followers of Christ but never put their faith into action.

Simply put, the book of James is an activist book. It details what people are supposed to do in order to further God's kingdom here on earth. How we are to **be doers of the word.** Not just merely a listener who listens. Not just a thinker who thinks. Not just a talker who talks. Not just a believer who believes. Nor just a prayer who prays from time to time.

But rather, we are to be doers, who have actions that exemplify Christ-like behaviors. More specifically, we are to be a believer of Christ, a doer of Christ, someone who gets things done for Christ and the kingdom of God.

I read a book recently that speaks of this same kind of doing, this same kind of active faith. The book is called, *Love Does*.

Love Does, is a book written by a gentleman by the name of Bob Goff. It is an exceedingly inspiring book as it details the life of Bob Goff and how he stops at nothing short of continuously offering love to people.

Each chapter is another way and another encounter with someone who Bob displays this love to.

In this book Bob writes about the kind of love "that doesn't just stop at thoughts and feelings. Bob's love is an attitude that takes action."

Bob's love **does**, hence the book title.

In this book, Bob goes into detail about how, "When Love does, then life gets very interesting and each day turns into a hilarious, whimsical, meaningful chance to put your faith into real action. It makes your faith more than something we talk about. It turns it into real life application."

Just to share a glimpse of this book and Bob's life with you, I'll share a short story from the 3rd chapter of the book.

The 3rd chapter is titled, Ryan in Love.

Bob starts out this chapter by talking about how he has a house down by the water front. How there is a little grassy path where couples hold hands and meander along the bay front right in his backyard.

He talks about how Bob and his wife enjoying sitting out on their back porch watching the couples stroll by.

Well one-night Bob and his wife were out there on the porch and a gentleman came strolling down the path. The man waved to Bob and his wife, and so they waved back, but instead of waving briefly and strolling on, the man kept waving.

So, Bob kept waving.

They kept waving to each other to the point where it became a little bit awkward. At that point the gentleman made his way up to Bob's back porch and he introduced himself.

He looked at Bob and his wife and he said: "Hi, my name is Ryan and I am in love."

Bob replied, "Well Ryan, that is just great! Congratulations!"

"No, no, that is not why I came over", Ryan shot back.

He said, "What I wanted to say is that, I walk by your house all the time and I have this girlfriend, you see, and I wanted to know……" he had a long pause then proceeded.

"I wanted to know if it would be okay If I asked my girlfriend to marry me in your backyard?"

Bob, a little caught off guard by all this, smiled and said, "Well of course you can Ryan! I think that sounds like a fantastic idea!"

Ryan replied, "Really? That's great!" and he left from Bob's back porch half-skipping and half-floating down the waterfront pathway.

A few days later Bob and his wife were sitting on their back porch and again they saw Ryan making his way towards them. Ryan didn't have his girlfriend with him, so Bob yelled form the porch, "Where's your other half Ryan?"

Ryan approached the porch and he said, "Well you know how I am going to propose in your backyard? Well, I was wondering if you thought it would be possible for us...." Ryan had another long pause and started stammering a bit.

Then he said, "well I was wondering if you thought it would be possible for us to have dinner on your back porch before I pop the big question?"

Bob, in his book, writes about how he had to bite his tongue to keep from laughing out loud. He talks about how he had never met Ryan before that week, and now he was asking if he could have a marriage proposal and dinner on his back porch.

Instead of laughing Bob fired back and said, "What the heck! Of course, you can have dinner on my back porch! Ryan, that is a great idea! What can I make for you two for dinner!?"

Ryan didn't even answer the question. He was beyond elated. He just turned around and started to skip and float his way down the pathway again.

Again a few days later Ryan showed up at the house. Solo. He approached Bob with a generic greeting and then his typical long pregnant pause, followed up with some stammering before he finally got his words out.

"Mr..... would it be possible for me to have some of my friends here to serve us when we are having dinner on your porch?"

Bob shot back, "You bet! What a great idea! How many would it take to serve you two dinner?"

Ryan responds with a sheepish, "20?"

Bob clearly taken aback by all of these audacious requests, is wonderfully stunned that Ryan wants 20 of his closest friends in his house to serve him and his girlfriend dinner. In his book he writes, "Now that's service, but when love does, love does it big!"

So Bob responded to Ryan's third request the same way he had each time. He said, "What a great idea Ryan! 20 it is!"

The next night Bob saw Ryan walking up the path again. Bob called out, "How are the plans coming?"

Ryan responded by saying, "Well, I was actually wondering if it would be okay if after dinner, and after my friends have left, if you could put some speakers on the porch and maybe my girlfriend and I could slow dance a bit?"

Of course, you want to dance on a stranger's porch, Bob thought to himself, and then he responded by saying, "Speakers it is!" He then asked if there was anything else, he could do for him?

Ryan said, "No I think that about covers it" and proceeded to skip and float down the path once more.

A day goes by, Ryan comes sprinting up the path towards Bob. Bob yells out, "How is it going Ryan?"

Ryan, who is out of breath says, "a boat….Mr. do you have a boat?"

At this point Bob is belly-laughing, and he asks him to repeat what he thought he had heard Ryan say.

"Do you have a boat", Ryan repeated.

"Well actually I do Ryan", Bob said.

And Ryan said, "Well can I borrow it?"

Bob says, "Okay Ryan, the boat is yours!"

He said, "I will take you and your girlfriend out on my boat after dinner at my house, after your 20 friends finish serving you, and after you slow dance together on my back porch. Then you can pop the question to your girlfriend on the front of my boat!"

"Great", Ryan said and floated away!

Believe it or not that was the last of Ryan's outlandish requests. A few nights later the BIG night came, and everything was in place.

Ryan and his girl came walking down the path hand in hand.

They approached Bob's house. His girlfriend began questioning why they were trespassing on this man's property. Ryan didn't say a word and just led her across the lawn toward a candle lit table on the porch. From there, they were served dinner by 20 of their closest friends.

Afterwards, they slow danced together on the porch and then made their way to the boat.

Bob took the couple out to the middle of the bay. To the exact spot where Bob and Ryan had agreed to position the boat, so Ryan could pop the question.

Turns out Ryan had fifty or more of his friends on the shore handle candles that spelled out the words, Will you marry me?

Ryan's girlfriend, floored by the whole evening and all the elaborate preparations yells, "**yes of course!**"

As soon as she said yes, the coast guard, who were positioned all around them, shot off every water cannon they had on their rigs to celebrate.

Bob had lined up that extra little bit with the coast guard to just add a little more flare, because that is what love does.

It does.

Love says yes to outlandish requests, requests that may inconvenience you. Love goes above and beyond to make other people feel loved and thought of and cared for, in a big big way.

It's the kind of love, **the kind of doing,** that isn't just with words and thoughts, but rather is shown with genuine actions and deeds!

At the end of chapter 3, Bob reflected more on his interaction with Ryan, he said:

"I don't know if God was a little bit like Ryan when He created everything, or if Ryan was a little bit like God. But what I do know is that Ryan's audacious love is some of the best evidence I've found of the kind of love Jesus talked about. A love that never grows tired or is finished finding ways to fully express itself."

He went on further to say, "I reflect on the "do" part of faith. That is because love is never stationary. In the end, love doesn't just keep thinking about it or keep planning for it. Simply put, love does."

This book, *Love Does*, echoes the words of James found in this passage.

This first chapter of James is an admonishment to get out there in the world. To become living, acting agents of Christ's love and grace to those who need it the most.

It is a passage that encourages us to get beyond ourselves and to put our faith into action. To live our faith out loud every day and in every circumstance. It is an admonishment to do the work of Christ.

This passage, this admonishment is intended to inform and direct our everyday lives where we are doers and not just merely hearers of God's word.

In the name of the Father, the Son and the Holy Spirit. Amen.

No Partiality
James 2:1-10; 14-18

This week is our second week diving into the Book of James. As I mentioned last week, we are spending about 5 weeks exploring and diving deeper into the book of James.

We are taking the next 5 weeks to take a closer look at who James was, what he had to say at the time, and how James' words still speak to us this day.

Last week we discussed how the book of James is an activist book. How James was calling the early disciples into action. To not just merely say they were Christians and followers of Christ, but to really put those words into practice.

Moreover, to put their faith into action.

This week we encountered the same kind of admonishment. The same kind of call where James was telling those early disciples to put their faith into action, **by loving their neighbor.**

In this passage James goes into a little bit more detail about that admonishment and delineates **how we are** to put our faith into action by loving our neighbor.

More specifically, he tells us that we are to love all our neighbors by not demonstrating any sort of partiality amongst them. By not demonstrating any sort of favoritism amongst them.

He says, that the love we display for each of our neighbors should be the same across the board, without any sort of distinction.

In this passage, James illustrated this admonishment by sharing a story about a man who entered a synagogue dressed very nicely and juxtaposes that with an individual who enters the synagogue dressed very poorly, with tattered clothing.

James states that it would be a sin for the people of that synagogue to show partiality and favoritism towards the person that is dressed more nicely. For them to show partiality towards the well dressed gentleman by being more hospitable or more kind towards him, while telling the person with torn clothing to go sit off to the side, or even worse to sit at their feet, as if he were only worthy to be a foot stool.

In this passage James underscores how our human tendency, sometimes, is to want to show favoritism to some individuals, while other times we do not demonstrate the same type of love and kindness to others.

He is highlighting how sometimes it is easier for us to show partiality to those who look nice, those who smell nice, and have a cheerful disposition, while other times it is easy to toss people to the side because they look and act differently than us.

In this passage we find a call **to treat all of God's children equally and fairly across the board.** A call to never differentiate between the love and care and hospitality we extend to our neighbors.

Recently, I was in my hometown Roanoke, VA and I came across this picture that was displayed outside of a church in the Grandin Court Village.

This picture, this sign, it illustrates the same message James was speaking of in this passage. The same call to love each of our neighbors equally across the board.

It speaks to the way in which we are to extend God's love and kindness and hospitality to each of God's children.

How there is to be no separation, no favoritism, no partiality in the way we love **each of neighbors.**

There is a cute little Turkish tale that I came across some years back, which also speaks to this.

The title of the Turkish tale is called, *The Hungry Coat*. *The Hungry Coat* is about a man named, Nasruddin.

Nasruddin is a Turkish man who owns a lot of land. He spends a lot of his time out in his fields working the land. One day, Nasruddin had been out in the fields tilling the ground, working the fields and the day had gotten away from him.

Day was quickly turning to night. Dusk was approaching, and he knew he had to be at a big dinner banquet at his neighbor's home that evening.

So Nasruddin, who was very famished from working all day, headed to the feast just the way he was dressed. He was fearful that if he headed home to shower and change his clothes then he would risk being late and consequently insult the host.

So Nasruddin, in his sweaty and mud stained work attire, headed to the banquet.

Upon arriving, the wealthy banquet host opened the door and instead of greeting

Nasruddin warmly, giving him a hug, and ushering him into his home, the host gave him a once over and snubbed him.

He walked away smugly and just left the door open, leaving Nasruddin to shut the door behind him and follow in-suit.

Nasruddin did just that, he entered the home feeling a little awkward. He shut the door behind him, and walked down the long foyer to the banquet hall.

As Nasruddin entered the hall, he joined the throngs of people who were already there and were very nicely dressed for the event. They all were looking very nice, and smelled very nice. The women had on long ballroom dresses with their hair all done up. The men had on tuxes with long tails.

Nasruddin, feeling exceedingly out of place now, sat down at the dinner table that was covered with nice linens. He scanned the table and saw all sorts of elaborate dishes that had been prepared.

As Nasruddin sat down to eat, he noticed that none of the dinner guests were greeting him. No one was asking him his name, what he did for a living, or asking questions like where he lived. They were all ignoring him.

Nasruddin, feeling very off-put by this whole encounter, feeling very awkward and uncomfortable, got up from the dinner table and without saying a word, and before he ever even took one bite of food, he walked out of the banquet hall and left the home.

Nasruddin, still very famished from a hard day's work, drives home. He takes a shower. He puts on his expensive cologne, he does is hair, he puts on his gold rings, his finest clothing, including a very expensive sports coat, and he drives back over to the dinner banquet.

This time as Nasruddin is greeted at the door by the dinner host, he is greeted with a smile and a warm embrace.

The dinner host says, "Nasruddin, come in…come in!"

As Nasruddin makes his way to the table people start to scoot over and make room for him to sit next to them. They very politely and lovingly pass him plates of food, so he can enjoy the elaborate meal that was prepared.

They tell him about their selves. They ask him questions like, what kind of work he does, where he lives, and so on.

Nasruddin, being the gracious man he was, he answers them all very politely and responds to each person kindly.

As it came time to eat, Nasruddin piled on his plate all kinds of Turkish delights. He loaded his plate full of lentils, chickpeas, falafels, hummus. On another plate he piled high the best of the desserts: figs, dates and baklava.

As Nasruddin prepared to take a bit of his food, he took those items one by one and he began to feed them to his coat.

One falafel at a time, one scoop of hummus at time, one piece of baklava at time. One bite at a time he would open his coat and place them in the pockets of his very expensive sports coat.

The glares abounded.

People were wide eyed from one end of the table to the next. People had their mouths hanging open as they watched all this taking place until finally someone spoke up.

Finally, someone cried out and said, "What exactly are you doing?" "Why are you feeding your coat in this manner?"

Nasruddin looked over and addressed the question.

He said:

"Well, when I first came to this feast in my old stinky sweaty farming clothes, I was not welcome.

No one would even speak to me.

But when I went home and showered and changed into my expensive clothes and changed into this coat, suddenly I was greeted warmly.

Nasruddin said, "So I realized it was not me that was welcome at this party, but my clothing.

And so, I am feeding my coat."

That is the tale of the Hungry Coat.

It is a pretty funny story. It is also pretty applicable to our lesson from James this morning. It captures what James was saying to the early church.

How he was calling them to not show partiality. To not show favoritism. To not distinguish between dinner guests. To not distinguish between any of God's children for any reason.

Sadly, James words remain true and valid to us this day. We continue to fall short of this call at times. Hard as we might try, sometimes it is difficult to not form judgements against others.

It is hard to not show favoritism towards people that are more like us. Those who we may have more in common with. Those who look like us and act like us.

Hard as we might try, sometimes it is hard to not favor one neighbor over the next.

Our call, as Christians, is to love our neighbors equally, fairly, and without any sort of distinction or partiality.

It is a call to love those who don't look like us, those who don't think like us, those who don't speak like we do, those who don't pray in the same way we do, or vote the same way we do.

Our call is to love our neighbors without hesitation and without exception.

I wanted to share one other story with you. This one is about an encounter that I had in Western NY.

While living up in NY, I was the Pastor for a beautiful church that was located in the middle of their quaint downtown.

It was a very old and well-established church, with beautiful gothic style architecture.

Huge steeples, massive sanctuary, big organ behind the chancel. People prided themselves on the beauty of this church. And rightfully so, this church was utterly breathtaking!

This church building, with its high steeples and beautiful gothic architecture, was a focal point of the downtown and highly photographed.

In this town, there was a gentleman who was homeless. There was not a large homeless population in this area, so this gentleman was known far and wide. Now, this gentleman was also a very kind man. He had a heart of gold and would talk to you for hours about God and his faith.

Often times, this man would sleep on the steps of the church. Especially during hot summer nights. Mostly because the steps of that church were stone, so it would help keep him cool on those hotter summer nights.

I also think he liked to sleep on those steps because he felt welcome there. Myself and some of the other parishioners of that church made him feel welcome. We would go over and talk to him during the day. We would ask him how his day was going, and what he had been up to. We treated him like we would any other friend or acquaintance. We would sometimes leave food out for him and made sure he had what he needed.

Well I started to receive had written notes from people in the community, and I started to receive anonymous phone calls and voicemails at the church about this man sleeping on the church stairs.

The crux of these messages was that it was "a bad look" for the church. That having a homeless man sleeping on the steps of that beautiful church was not acceptable or appropriate. That the church should be more concerned about it's image and reputation, rather than allowing some vagrant to find shelter there.

Now it would be pretty hypocritical to be a church, and to profess to be a haven, a refuge and a sanctuary for people to only then usher them away because we were more concerned about an image or a reputation.

It would be pretty sad to be this big beautiful church, known in and throughout the town, to only then shun some of it's neighbors away.

It would have been sad if the elders of that church would have responded to those letters and those voicemails by agreeing with those individuals who had made their complaints.

It would have been exceedingly sad if the church elders had decided to show partiality and favoritism to some of their neighbors while casting others aside.

But that is not what happened.

The elders of that church, and the rest of the congregation continued to demonstrate love, and hospitality, and kindness to that man. They chose to love their neighbor without distinction or partiality.

That is what James was talking about in this passage.

Not favoring the "more elite." Not favoring the people who we think are elite. Not demonstrating partial treatment towards those who dress nicer, those who smell nice, those who look more like "us".

James' word to us this day remain a true and valid reminder to get out there in the world and to be activists.

To put our faith into action by demonstrating love and acceptance, kindness and hospitality to all of our neighbors.

May we all heed James' call to us this day. His call to love each of our neighbors the same across the board. Equally, fairly, and without any sort of partiality.

In the name of the Father, the Son and the Holy Spirit. Amen.

The Power of Words
James 3:1-12

As you all know and are well aware, this is our third week of focusing on the book of James.

This is the third week in our 5-week series where we are taking a closer look at this book. Exploring who James was, what he had to say, and how his words remain true and valid to us this present day.

For the past couple weeks, we have explored and discussed how the book of James is an activist book. We have discussed how out of the 108 verses that the book of James contains, over 60 of those verses are call verses.

They are call verses or admonishments to get up, to get out in the world and to put our faith into action.

Essentially, they are call verses to go out into the world and to do work for the kingdom of God.

The first week we explored the call to get out in the world and to take care of the widows and the orphans. To be doers of God's word, not just merely hearers. To be doers by being living and acting agents of Christ's love and grace in this world.

Last week we explored further the call to love your neighbor, and **how we are to do just that.**

How we are to love each of our neighbors equally, fairly, without any sort of distinction or partiality.

This week we have a call to keep our tongues in check.

It is a call to control our speech and to use it to build up the kingdom of God, not to tear down or harm the kingdom of God, here on earth.

In this passage, James goes into detail about how dangerous our mouths can be at times. How dangerous the tongue can become and the far-reaching damage that can occur because of the words that we form.

In this passage James uses three different metaphors to illustrate this point. Each metaphor explores a different aspect of the tongue. Each is a metaphor for the power of human speech.

First, James starts out with a metaphor about a horse and a bridle. For those of you who are more familiar with horses and riding equipment, then you know that the bridle is the riding component that directs the speed, the direction, and the strength of the horses' pull.

The bridle, which is incidentally placed inside of the horse's mouth, functions by pressing against the horse's tongue.

Quite literally then, the one who can control the horse's tongue, with the bridle in its mouth, is able to control the whole animal.

Able to control and direct the speed of the horse. The direction the horse goes in, and the strength or intensity of the horse's pull.

The second comparison that James makes regarding the tongue, is by comparing it to a rudder of a ship.

He says, "Look at ships: though they are so large that it takes strong winds to drive them, yet they are guided by a very small rudder wherever the will of the pilot directs."

The metaphor of the ship's rudder drives home the same point that James was making with the horse's bridle. The captain of the ship, the rudder, and the ship itself are comparable to the rider, the bit and bridle, and the horse.

They illustrate how these large objects, a ship or a horse, are controlled by a very small component and by a person. They are controlled by the person who oversees steering each one, which leads us right into the third metaphor.

Thirdly, James draws comparisons of the tongue by likening it to a small fire.

He says, "how great a forest is set ablaze by a small fire, and the tongue is a fire."

Again, it is another metaphor for how such a small entity, much like the bit and bridle, and much like the rudder of ship, can have large, widespread effects.

James, as a person was very focused on the damaging effects that our speech can have on other people, and consequently the widespread effects that it can have on the kingdom of God.

As I mentioned before, there are 108 verses in the book of James. 46 of those verses touch on matters of speech, language, words, and the importance of choosing our words wisely. That is 43% of this book. That is nearly half of the entire book of James that focuses on speech and the words we use.

James was very concerned about how the early church was using their speech in their everyday lives. He was highlighting the effects that it can have on those around us and how quickly damage can spread to far reaching areas.

I think we have ample supporting evidence to back up and validate James' claim, that our words have the potential to be lethal.

That **our words have power.**

Our words can exclude or embrace. They can heal or humiliate. They can lift up or tear down.

And as Christians, our words ought to be healing words. They ought to bring grace and peace. They should build up and not tear down. They should heal rather than harm. We should speak words of encouragement, rather than words of discouragement.

Recently, I came across a study that was conducted by a gentleman by the name of, Masaru Emoto.

Masaru Emoto is a Japanese scientist who performed some interesting experiments on the effect that words have. More specifically, the energy or the power behind our words.

He started a string of experiments back in the early 1990's and in one of his experiments he found that: when water that's free from all impurities is frozen, it will form beautiful ice crystals that look exactly like snowflakes under a microscope.

Conversely, water that is polluted or has additives, like fluoride, will freeze without forming crystals.

In his experiment, Emoto took pure water. Water without any sort of additives, pure water that when frozen should form these beautiful ice crystals that would look like snowflakes under the microscope.

He poured that pure water into various vials. Some of those vials were labeled with negative phrases like, I hate you and fear. Some of the other vials were labeled with positive phrases like, I love you and peace.

After 24 hours, the water had become completely frozen and the vials that were labeled with the negative phrases did not possess any sort of beautiful crystallization under the microscope. Instead, it yielded gray, misshapen clumps.

In contrast, the vials that were labeled with more positive phrases like, I love you and peace, after 24 hours of being frozen, they produced gleaming beautiful and perfectly hexagonal crystals.

Emoto's experiment proved that energy is generated by positive or negative words. It scientifically proves how our words can change the physical structure of an object.

The results of his experiments are detailed in a series of books beginning with, *The Hidden Messages in Water*, where you can see the astounding before and after photos of these incredible water crystals.

Just to share one other fascinating experiment that Emoto conducted, this time he tested the power of spoken words.

He placed two cups of cooked white rice in two separate mason jars and tightened the lids on both jars.

Then he labeled the jars. One jar he labeled, "Thank You" and on the other jar he labeled, "You Fool."

The jars were left in an elementary school classroom, and the students were instructed to speak the words on the labels to the corresponding jars twice a day.

After 30 days of doing this, the rice in the jar that was constantly insulted, the jar that was labeled "you fool", had shriveled into a black, gelatinous mass.

Contrastingly, the rice in the jar that was thanked daily and spoken to with words of encouragement was as white and fluffy as the day it was made. It was a dramatic example and a dramatic display of the impact our words have and the power behind our words.

Our words have power, and they most certainly have an impact on those around us.

They can either build up or tear down. They can heal, or they can harm. They can encourage, or they can discourage and destroy.

I am sure many of us have had our own personal encounters with the power of our words and the dramatic effect that they can have on others. I am sure we have seen the effects that words spoken in anger, and words spoken out of frustration can have on other people.

I was sharing a similar story about this topic early this week. I was telling a couple of parishioners about an instance when I was maybe 8 or 9 years old.

I wanted to go outside and play with my friends, ride bikes, make a fort in the woods, do whatever kids did back in that day and age, before smart phones and social media.

Well, my father had a very different idea about how I was supposed to spend my afternoon. He did not want me outside playing. Instead he wanted me inside, cleaning.

He wanted me to straighten my room up and get prepared for school the next morning.

And I remember looking up at him as an 8 or 9-year-old little girl and screaming at the top of my lungs, "**I hate you!**"

Well, before I could turn around and stomp off. I saw the visible effect that those spoken words had on my father.

I watched my 6-foot-tall father shrink to about 5 feet. I could visible see sadness sweep across my father's face as those words I had spoken out of selfish anger penetrated his heart.

You could almost audibly hear a little bit of his heart break.

To see that happen. To see the visible effect that the power of my words had on him and the impact that phrase had on him, tore me apart.

Instead of flipping around and stomping off, I started apologizing profusely. I most certainly started cleaning my room and began straightening my room up, with a smile on my face.

But more importantly, that was an extremely important lesson that I learned at a very young age.

A lesson learned about never using the phrase; I hate you, to anyone, for any reason. But it was also a lesson about the impact our words can have and the power of our words. The effect our words can have on others and the far-reaching damage our words can cause.

There are many a times we find ourselves in difficult situations, painful, hurtful conversations, heated arguments and during those times we retaliate. We react out of a place anger or frustration and we end up saying things that we later wished we hadn't.

That was the point of James' letter this morning. To realize that our tongue, small as it might be, is powerful beyond measure. It steers, directs and leads a person's life. Likewise, it has the power to set ablaze a whole forest, if we let it.

So, the lasting question from this passage is, how do we not let it?

How do we prevent ourselves from allowing such a small member of our body not destroy us or those around us?

How do we prevent our tongue of fire from setting the whole forest ablaze?

And to answer that question I would like to introduce to you the philosophy of Pause and Pray.

When in doubt…pause and pray.

When angry…. pause and pray.

When tried, stressed, hot, and hangry: pause and pray.

We could keep adding to this list of scenarios in which we may not react to someone with the most cheerful disposition or the most edifying words.

The whole idea is to pause during that time. To allow a little time, a little separation, some space between the moment when one person's words hit our ears and cause an emotional sting, till the time that we offer our response.

The idea is to practice the pause during that time, and to pray during that pause.

To Pray for God's words. To pray for God's wisdom.

To pray for Christ's peace to enter your body, and to pray for Christ's grace to leave your body, through your spoken word.

It's like the age old saying, "think before you speak", or "if you don't have anything nice to say then don't say anything at all."

There is wisdom in these age-old sayings.

However, centuries before these sayings were created and passed down, our desert fathers had their own similar sayings.

The desert fathers were early Christian hermits, ascetics and monks who mainly lived in the desert of Egypt beginning around the 3rd century. Silence and stillness were essential practices of the early desert mothers and fathers.

Some of their ancient wisdom includes sayings from Father Agathon who once said, that for three years he lived with a stone in his mouth, until he had learned to keep silence.

And Father Poemen who also said, "The victory over all the afflictions that befall you is to keep silence.'" A brother asked Father Poemen one time, 'Is it better to speak or to be silent?' The old man said to him, 'The man who speaks for God's sake does well, but he who is silent for God's sake also does well.'

Father Sisoes once said, "Even to the point of death, monks should control themselves so as not to speak."

Just To bring it a little more current, Benjamin Franklin once said, "Remember not only to say the right thing in the right place, but far more difficult still, to leave unsaid the wrong thing at the tempting moment."

Practice the pause.

In the name of the Father, the Son, and the Holy Spirit. Amen.

Submit Yourselves
James 3:13-4:3;7-8a

This week is our 4th week diving into the book of James. As you know, for the past several weeks we have taken a closer look at who James was, what he had to say and how his book still remains very relevant to us in our present everyday lives.

For the past few weeks, we have talked about how the book of James is an activist book. How James was calling the early Christians to put their faith into action. To take the teachings of Christ and put them into real life practice.

James was writing to encourage the early church to consistently live-out what they had learned in Christ. He wanted his readers to mature in their faith in Christ by living-out what they said they believed in their everyday lives.

Throughout his letter to those early Christians, and throughout the topics and chapters we have discussed in the weeks prior, we heard James telling those early Christians to live their faith out by caring for the widows and the orphans. That is to say, that they were to live their faith out by caring for those who are marginalized, those who were oppressed, suffering, and in need.

In previous chapters, James also wrote about the importance of loving our neighbors. Loving them equally and fairly. He wrote about the importance of not distinguishing between our neighbors. Not showing partiality to some, while withholding God's love and grace and kindness to others.

As we discussed last week, James focused a lot on the importance of our speech, our language, the words that we choose to use with people. James was very concerned about the way in which the early church was treating one another with their language and speech.

He reminds them of the importance of speaking words of grace and peace to others. And not allowing our tongue or our speech to hinder our relationships with other people or hinder the kingdom of God.

Throughout the book of James, it is one admonishment after the next. One call after the next. A call to rise up and put our faith into action. To put our faith into practice with the highest of ideals.

This week is no different within the book of James. Our passage this morning contains the sternest admonishment of them all.

It is the admonishment to submit ourselves to God.

Some may wonder what an actual submission to God would entail. What that would look like. How one would go about submitting oneself to God.

And I'm sure there are a variety of answer for those questions.

But in its most basic sense, an actual submission to God, simply means to yield to God's ways. To surrender your will, your plans, your desires and aspirations for your life, to God.

We are to submit to God, by aligning our plan and will for our lives with God's plan and will for our lives.

This word, submission simply means, the act of submitting to a higher authority. Submitting control to another. The condition of being submissive means being humble and compliant.

Now, I say this is one of the more sterner admonishments within the book of James because James was serious and unrelenting about the fact that, as a Christian, part of the faith journey, part of the faith walk, means and entails submitting to the Lord.

As Christians, part of the faith walk entails constantly submitting and yielding our plans, our ways, our will to God over and over again.

James knew this was a hard thing to do and that it took constant work and devotion for someone to truly submit to the Lord.

That is why he went into so much detail about what happens when a person does or does not submit their ways to the Lord.

In this passage James talks about how, the person who truly has submitted to God experiences bliss in their lives.

More specifically, he illustrates this notion by juxtaposing a person's life who has sought after true wisdom, verse the person who has sought after false wisdom.

He delineates how the person who has sought after true wisdom, that being the wisdom of God, and has constantly sought to align their life with God's will, will in-turn experience peace in their lives.

James points out how their life will be marked with gentleness and mercy. Their actions will be deeds of good fruits.

He says, it is the person who has sought after true wisdom and submitted themselves to God, that will experience the good life.

Similarly, James also goes into detail about the other individual, who has not submitted or yielded to God's ways.

He describes this person as the one who has sought after false wisdom.

He says, you will know the individual who has sought after false wisdom in life, because their life will be marked with bitter envy. Selfish ambition will rule in their hearts.

They will be boastful, and their actions will be displays of wickedness of every kind.

Essentially what James was saying here, what he was pointing out in this passage, was that there are two ways to go through life.

1. You can either submit yourselves to God. You can submit and yield your ways, your plans, your aspirations to God and align your will with God's plan and will for your life.

or 2. You can ignore his advice and suggestion, and forge your own way in life, on your own.

In illustrating these two paths that person can take in life, he delineates the pros and cons of each one.

He delineates how tough and difficult life will be, and will continue to become, if one chooses not to yield to God. While on the other hand, he points out how great and wonderful life can be when one does choose to submit, and yield themselves to God.

James says it is in choosing to submit to God's plans and God's desires for your life, that you will truly be able to have and enjoy the Good Life.

Last fall I decided to take a walk. It was a two-week long walk and it was 161 miles long. It stretched from Porto, Portugal to Santiago, Spain.

This walk, this hike, I took is commonly referred to as the Camino de Santiago. It is also referenced as, "the way of St. James". It is referenced as "the way of St. James", because the places along this hike are all places that St. James traversed as he preached the gospel in and throughout those areas.

The end point of the hike is the city of Santiago. The name Santiago is a name that way back in the day was derived from the Latin term, Sancti Iacobi, which translates as "Saint James". So the actual ending point for the hike in Santiago, Spain means St. James.

In addition, the literal end point for the hike, are the steps of the Grand Cathedral in Santiago, Spain. This is the grand Cathedral where St. James' remains are believed to be buried.

What is very interesting and fascinating to me about this hike is that there are 5 different routes a person can take. 5 different routes, but you still end up at the exact same end point. You still end the hike on the steps of the grand Cathedral in Santiago, Spain.

In order to get to Santiago, you can either take the Northern way, which starts in the city of Irun on the border of France. That route it is about 827 km long.

Or you can take the French way, which is most popular, and very long. It takes about 6 weeks to hike and you hike through the Pyrenees mountains.

Or you can take what is called the Primitive way, which is the oldest route to Santiago and begins in a town called Oviedo on the coast of Spain. It is quite hilly and about 261 km.

Or you can take the Portuguese way, which is the second most popular route and starts in Lisbon, Portugal.

I took the coastal Portuguese route that started in Porto, Portugal. I hiked 161 miles along the coast of Portugal and Spain and when I reached the northern tip of Spain I cut into the interior of Spain, as I made my way down towards the city of Santiago.

I like to think that I took the more beautiful route as I had constant views of the sea to my left. Really gorgeous port towns I stayed overnight in. There were endless amounts of fresh seafood to enjoy, and just an overall tranquil setting with the beach surrounding me.

As I mentioned, there are all sorts of routes a person can take to reach Santiago. Coastal or mountainous. Flat or hilly. People can hike the interior or exterior of countries. A person can take a longer route or if they are limited on time, they can take one of the shorter routes. There is a variety of hikes or walks a person can take as they make their way along the Camino De Santiago.

During my 161-mile trek I had a lot of time on my hands, as you might imagine.

So, I did a lot of thinking. I did a lot of praying. I would say I was mostly only in conversation God, for the bulk of each day. But also, all along this trail I did a lot of people watching.

I would watch as people would pass me. I would notice how they had a lighter pack then I did, which allowed them to walk much quicker. I would notice the people I would pass, and note their fatigue or how they looked like they needed to stop for food or water.

Each day as I was out there hiking and walking the coast, I noticed the various types of people that were on this trail. Young and old, most people were much older. I would say the average hiker was in their 60's.

I noticed the various ethnicities of the hikers. There were people from all over the world that had come to hike this trail and to experience the "way of St. James".

As I people watched and noticed how all of us were so different in many varying ways, I also thought about all the other people that were on the 4 other trails.

On average, 1,000 people a day finish that hike. So, I thought about all those people that were traversing the same trail but coming from different directions, and how we would all end up at the same end point. On the stairs of that Grand Cathedral in Santiago.

What is so interesting and so fascinating to think about is, how so many people from various directions (Lisbon, the interior of Spain, the far corner of France) were all headed to the exact same place. But we were all having very different experiences on the same trail, as we each take our different routes.

Some were experiencing the expansive mountainous views of the Pyrenees

Mountain chain. Some were experiencing and traversing the more city like environments as they made their way up the interior of Spain. I was experiencing the beauty and bliss of the sea as I took the coastal route from Portugal.

Depending on which route a person took, it changed the day to day experiences. It changed the distance a person would have to hike, it could make their route shorter or longer depending on where they began.

It changed the type of terrain a person traversed. Whether it would be steep and mountainous or flat and coastal.

If a person took the less traveled route (the Primitive route) then there were fewer lodging accommodations, which meant a person must camp outside. Which then affected what you packed and brought with you.

Whichever route a person had chosen to take, it changed and shaped their days on that trail. It changed and shaped the experiences they would have along the trail. It could either enhance it or it had the potential to make the hike a little more difficult or a little more challenging.

It's a great visualization for what James was talking about in our passage this morning. There are different routes we can take in life. There are different trails we can take, but we are all going to end up at the same place. We are all going to end up in heaven, united with God for all of eternity.

Depending on the trail you pick, it will shape and effect your experiences here on earth. Depending on the trail you choose it will shape and define how easy life comes to you or how difficult life may become.

In this passage James speaks of two different routes you can take. You can take the route where you are seeking after false wisdom. Or you can take the route where you are seeking after true wisdom, divine wisdom.

The route of true wisdom, the trail we choose where we fully submit our lives, our will, our wants and desires and greatest hopes and aspirations to God, that route is sure to be marked with peace.

The route of false wisdom, as James tells us, entails a trail of hardship. It is marked with envy and selfish ambition. It entails never feeling truly satisfied in oneself. It is marked with disorder and wickedness of every kind, James says.

Both paths, both trails or routes, they will lead you to the same place, but there are gravely different experiences along the way.

Therefore, the lasting question from this passage of James then becomes: Which path do you choose? The path of true wisdom or the path of false wisdom?

In what ways do you still need to submit and yield your ways to the Lord, so that you can seek after the true wisdom?

What are you still hanging on to and controlling, that you need to hand over and yield to God?

These are all questions to ask ourselves as we further explore which path or trail we will choose to take in life.

In the name of the Father, the Son and the Holy Spirit. amen.

Pray Y'all
James 5:3-20

This week is our 5th and final week in the book of James. This week, like the weeks prior, centers upon another admonishment from James. It consists of another series of ways, in which we, as Christians and faithful followers of Christ, are to live or lives.

As you are well aware at this point, the book of James is a series of guidelines about how to tow the so-called, "Christian line". How we are to embody our faith with our everyday actions and not just simply profess our faith with our words.

Throughout the book of James, he is constantly and consistently calling out the early church on their inability to live their faith out-loud. He continues to evoke them to higher standards of living and interacting with others. Constantly admonishing them to live and act in such a way where Christ is emulated.

In this particular chapter of James, he is calling out his fellow brother and sisters on their lack of prayer. He reminds them that they are to pray during every season. They are to pray if they are happy. They are to pray if they are sick They are to pray if they are sad or in trouble, but most of all he reminds them that they are to pray for each other.

In this chapter he says,

Is anyone among you in trouble? Let them pray. Is anyone happy? Let them sing songs of praise. Is anyone among you sick? Let them call the elders of the church to pray over them and anoint them with oil in the name of the Lord. And the prayer offered in faith will make the sick person well; the Lord will raise them up. If they have sinned, they will be forgiven. Therefore, confess your sins to each other and pray for each other so that you may be healed.

James ends this admonishment by saying, the prayer of a righteous person is powerful and effective. And there are a couple reasons why James says it is powerful and effective.

The first reason it is powerful and effective is because it allows us to empty ourselves of all the burdens we may be carrying with us. It allows us to empty ourselves of whatever may be troubling us.

Similarly, prayer allows us to express our praises to God. To express our joy for the many blessings we have received. More importantly, it allows us to come before God and be still. It allows us to feel and experience the holy presence of God.

I wanted to share a pretty profound story with you regarding prayer.

Now, It is no secret that church attendance throughout our entire denomination is declining.

There are many people hard at work at the Presbyterian Headquarters in Louisville, KY working to address this issue. The department that focuses primarily on the issue of church decline in Louisville, is called the Evangelism and Church Growth Department.

I was fortunate enough to meet the director of this department a few years back and he shared a bit of information with me that I found to be quite interesting. He told me that every single day at 10:02 a.m. the entire office comes together for prayer.

So every single person puts down their pen, and whatever they are working on at the time, and they meet to pray for our denomination. They pray for all the churches that comprise each and every single one of our presbyteries, then they pray for our presbyteries and leaders, and they pray for our synods.

You may be curious as to why they do this at 10:02 a.m. every morning. I was curious about that myself and when I asked, I was told that 10:02 a.m. corresponds with the bible verse in Luke which states, **the harvest is plentiful, but the laborers are few, therefore ask the lord of the harvest to send out laborers into his harvest.**

I was shocked to hear that these high ranking professionals at the Presbyterian headquarters, would stop everything they were doing at 10:02 each day, so they could come together and pray.

It was so hard to fathom all these individuals putting their pens down, or stepping away from their computers, hanging up their phones, or ending their meetings early, so they could enter into prayer with God.

And It may be hard for us to imagine this occurring, and shocking to hear at first, but these are the type of behaviors and actions that should be taking place.

Praying for God's guidance on such an important issue. Praying for the churches that are facing difficult times, and praying for the leaders that govern them.

The fact that it was so shocking to hear that these individuals stopped what they were working on each day at 10:02 to pray, is also a good indication that we have gotten far away from the practice of prayer.

The simple fact that it is surprising that people would stop in the middle of their work morning to pray, is an indication that prayer is not a big enough priority in our daily lives. It is such thoughts as this, that makes James' admonishment in this passage even more timely in our present day lives.

Prayer is one of the major ways in which we access and nurture our living relationship with God, so it really should be more of a priority in our daily lives. It should take precedence over our work duties or the tasks at hand.

Taking time out of our busy and hectic lives every day to spend time in the living presence of God. Unburdening ourselves, making our prayer requests known, offering our praises to God, as well as asking for God's guidance in our lives. These are the things that maintain our living relationship with God and consequently enhances our lives.

There is one other benefit to prayer that I wanted to touch on, and that is that it invites us into a living relationship with one another. That is the other half of James' admonishment in this passage, as he told the early church to pray for one another.

With this admonishment James was helping the early church to create a community for themselves through the practice of prayer. As people come together to pray alongside one other and specifically for each other it creates a community. It lets people know that they are not alone, that someone is thinking of them, but it also alerts those individuals and that community to the needs of that individual. It helps others to know what is going on in that person's life.

I was down in a small lake town outside of Columbia, South Carolina several summers ago. Very cute and quaint lake community. While I was there, I had the opportunity to visit a Presbyterian Church.

This church was fairly large, probably 600 to 800 people on Sunday mornings, over 150 youth group students, and a children's ministry that was growing exponentially every week.

This church had only recently begun to experience so much growth, and in response to that growth they needed to build another building for the children's ministry.

The new building they had designed, which was solely for the children's ministry was 4.2 million dollars. I was completely shocked by the fact that the church was taking on this sort of expense in order to expand their children's ministry, but I was even more shocked when I saw how much money they had already raised for it. In just 8 months they had reached their targeted fund-raising goal, of 2.5 million. And that's when they told me about their main fund-raiser.

They had raised 2.5 million dollars by having stickers printed that said Pray Y'all. The stickers were the white oval stickers you see all the time that say, OBX, or Pawley's Island, or The Keys. You can insert any other beach location or destination you may be familiar with, most places have these white oval stickers printed up with their name or initials on them.

So this church did the same thing and had thousands and thousands of these white oval stickers printed that said, Pray Y'all! And they were selling like crazy!

The best part of this whole fund-raiser was that each time someone purchased one of these stickers that said Pray Y'all, they signed a pledge to pray for that church. More specifically to pray for the new building and the children's ministry of that church.

I cannot tell you how many cars I saw with this Pray Ya'll sticker on them. I saw them all throughout the quaint little lake community. I saw them stuck on the sides of boats when I was out on the lake. I saw them all around the city of Columbia, and even 2 hours outside of Columbia as I was heading back home to Virginia. These Pray Y'all stickers were everywhere.

This tells us two things: 1. We need to include this as one of our own fundraising techniques. And 2. it illustrates how prayer draws us into community with others.

This crafty little fundraising idea, to print up Pray Y'all stickers, had drawn this entire lake community together, and it had invited all the surrounding communities and cities to become part of their community through prayer, as well.

There is something very personal and intimate about making your prayer requests known and about praying for one another. It connects you with individuals in a deep and meaningful way. It draws people into community with one another and invites you into a real and authentic relationship with one another.

Prayer is an important part of our faith. It is how we access and nurture our relationship with God. It is one of the main ways in which we maintain our living relationship with God as it brings us into the living presence of God, but prayer also invites us into a living relationship with one another.

Just like the busy church officials working at the Presbyterian Headquarters in Louisville, prayer should be a priority and something we stop our busy hectic lives for, each and every day. And much like this little lake community in South Carolina, we should be inviting others into a living relationship with us through prayer, and creating a community for ourselves by praying for one another.

Or as James says in this passage, pray for each other so that you may be healed, because the prayer of a righteous person is powerful and effective.

In the name of the Father, the Son, and the Holy Spirit. Amen.

www.ingramcontent.com/pod-product-compliance
Lightning Source LLC
Chambersburg PA
CBHW052206110526
44591CB00012B/2097